Doubtful Harbor

The Hollis Summers Poetry Prize

GENERAL EDITOR: DAVID SANDERS

Named after the distinguished poet who taught for many years at Ohio University and made Athens, Ohio, the subject of many of his poems, this competition invites writers to submit unpublished collections of original poems. The competition is open to poets who have not published a book-length collection as well as to those who have.

Full and updated information is available on the Hollis Summers Poetry Prize web page: ohioswallow.com/poetry_prize

Doubtful Harbor

Poems

Idris Anderson

OHIO UNIVERSITY PRESS

ATHENS

Ohio University Press, Athens, Ohio 45701
ohioswallow.com
© 2018 by Idris Anderson
All rights reserved

Printed in the United States of America
Ohio University Press books are printed on acid-free paper ∞ ™

Cover photo: Doubtful Sound, New Zealand (courtesy of author)

28 27 26 25 24 23 22 21 20 19 18   5 4 3 2 1

Library of Congress Cataloging-in-Publication Data
Names: Anderson, Idris, author.
Title: Doubtful harbor : poems / Idris Anderson.
Description: Athens, Ohio : Ohio University Press, [2018] | Series:
The Hollis Summers poetry prize
Identifiers: LCCN 2017058085| ISBN 9780821423172 (paperback) |
ISBN 9780821446317 (pdf)
Subjects: | BISAC: POETRY / General. .
Classification: LCC PS3601.N5438 A6 2018 | DDC 811/.6–dc23
LC record available at https://lccn.loc.gov/2017058085

for

Diane Dyer Harmon

and

Suzanne

Contents

Three

Four

Woman in Kuala Lumpur

Jet-lagged, I arrived a day early and took a tour:
the Batu Caves, a pewter factory, a batik shop,
a rubber tree plantation, a bug shop.
Newly dead bugs dried and dipped in acetate,
glued to pins for lapels or shaped into objects
westerners would buy. It was foul.
Burned bugs and the cloy of acetate.
I got back on the bus.

The driver left me at a taxi stand. "Easy here,"
he said. "Easy." Rush hour, a long line.
I was in no hurry, people seemed nice,
business suits, valises, shopping bags.
I listened to conversations I couldn't understand,
day-chatter tones you'd find anywhere.
The eaters, the readers, the blank looking-ahead
faces, adolescents with electronic toys. At last,
at the front of the line, I said "Ampang Puteri,"
the hospital near my hotel. "The Garden," I said,
my hand on the door handle. The driver shook
his head. "Nuh," he said and looked beyond me.

This happened a third time.

To the woman next in line, Muslim I think—
her long everyday dress of flowers, a swath
of folded silk from shoulder to waist: "Good luck,"
I said and meant it, and saw beyond her in the crowd
two policemen in military garb, gold braid
and epaulets. I hoped they spoke enough

English to help me out. Or I'd find a phone,
call the hotel.

I heard her voice then, just a sound, no word
I understood. She was on the backseat
of the taxi, her hand moving in that universal
gesture summoning me. It was all gesture,
and tone, something in her voice,
and the meeting of eyes.
We had no language between us.

I went with her in the taxi through the smog and blare
of late afternoon traffic: motorcycle rev, the guttural
diesel and brake of stop-and-go trucks. My hotel not far,
a drop-off, I figured, on the way to her own destination.
Maybe out of the way entirely. I'll never know.
I paid the driver what he said and some extra odd coins.

The woman—I could see now she was old
and beautiful, deep lines in her face, as though
she'd earned them—had slid over the seat to where
I'd just sat. As the car pulled off, we both
opened our hands on the window between us,
all the fingers and thumbs matching up.

I who have had faith in language, what the sentence
can say, one human to another—it's clumsy,
the telling of this story which should be a song
without words, oboe and strings perhaps,
a ballet of gesture, grace of the body itself,
a language I don't know but desire,
without the heat and noise of words.

One

Painting the Bathroom

I'm getting the hang of it, drawing the line
without level or square, green next to white,
blue next to green. Edge the crown, the corners.
Brush and caulk freehand, without blue tape.
In his splotchy white overalls, the professional painter
told his secrets: keep your brush loaded,
lay it on, keep it wet, one or two strokes, that's it.
Given time, given space. Easier said than done.
Altogether elsewhere, north, in a house by the sea,
the landscape's all circles and arcs. No, to be exact,
it's inexact squiggles—tangles, and unexpected
headland hills undulating, a shore of irregular
marshes and marsh flats, blurry margins all around
in six rectangular windows, a sheen on the water.

I learned to paint by numbers, two Pomeranians,
eight plastic rounds of oily colors. In the beginning,
it was nothing but faint blue lines on cardboard,
obsessive hairy streaks of white and tan.
One thing, I discovered, could become another.
Now it's all Rothko and Benjamin Moore, soft
but definitive box squares of Cloud White,
Tapestry Beige (a kind of fresh light celery),
Hale Navy on the vanity with the white knobs.
Colors of matter gathered from the landscape.
Earth, pollen, weed tucked into an apron,
ground, boiled, mixed in a mud hut.
Pots and walls colored with the potions.
First cause of all beauty beyond knowing.

Slow day here. Fog settled in. What I thought
was a marsh hawk is, closer, a vulture, wheeling
and tilting. Nothing's dead yet. Tiny people,
a couple? a father and daughter? are walking the spit.
Their dog off leash runs ahead, waits for the humans,
who ignore him. They must be talking. He runs again.
It's too soon for the kitesurfers I saw yesterday,
four of them under power-red curves catching good air.
I've become a contemplative, of textures, of what
I can feel between finger and thumb, of what happens
that is not balance or clarity, that comes not from
knowledge or training, that is at the edges of mystery
where light is changed and water tidal, where dark
green jags of cypresses mass along Bodega Bay.

Swan-Boat Ride

*from a fragmented draft of an Elizabeth Bishop poem
never completed*

In the Boston Public Gardens
when I was three, a *live swan paddled*
among artificial birds, *pontoons* fitted
with tall wood wings and yellow *pedals.*
The white paint peeled like feathers.

As our boat drifted in the *dead water,*
my mother's hand meddled idle
in the wet — dirty, cold, and black,
then *proffered a peanut* from a sack.
A thing to do to amuse a daughter.

Ungracious, terrifying bird!
Apparently it had not heard
that it's unkind, cruel to attack
a woman dressed in blackest black,
as widows do; she was my mother too.

"See," she said to me (it's all she said),
her black kid glove split and red.
I saw the hole, the drop of *blood,*
the hissing beak, the mark of teeth,
the finger's flesh, the *amniotic flood.*

Afloat, afloat, atilt the boat,
the whole pond swayed —

breath *suspends and death descends*
and *madness* comes

to *flower beds* so bright and trim,
to *the State of Massachusetts seal,*
the State House Dome, its thinly crusted sun.

In that dream I dream again,
my mother lifts her veil
to kiss me, a *pattern*ed lace I memorized—
her fading face and fragile eyes—
fine and dark and real.

Shucks

in memoriam, Alice Brice

In a bar in Boston, somewhere near the aquarium,
gentlemen in white coats shucked oysters. We sipped
cold brine, a taste not of heaven but of earth,
and the oyster, loosened, slipped from the clean inside
of the shell, no human hand or finger ever touching,
just the lip, then the tongue, then the teeth in that soft flesh,
the one chewy button of muscle. Alice ordered
Campari "with lots of lime." "One for me too," I said.
Among memories of reading Keats on the lawns
of the Yard that summer, I keep this one. The bitter red drink
she called for years later in Santa Fe. Just a weekend.
After persuading me to buy a red cape from a woman
in the market, we settled into a late lunch at the Pink Adobe,
sipping, shucking our stories. The last time I saw her.

Red Oaks

I wake to trees in a window
or rather four windows
like a Japanese screen,
each panel a version
of a New Hampshire wood.

It's winter white under the trees,
a ground like crumpled silk
or parchment flecked
with fibers of rag—
the litter of stump and stone.

And though morning is not brilliant
and there is no sound and nothing
is moving, I know
under the mounds of soft snow
are rivulets of melt refrozen,

layers of hard black leaves,
white roots growing
quietly, quietly.
A few stiff leaves cling,
the color of grocery-bag paper.

The subject is trees—
tall-slender or scrub-bent,
brown-gray against
white sky. A heavy stroke
across the four windows—

a hardwood fallen,
rotted orange, its bark
curled sheets sloughed off,
its thick stump splintered,
the red blond of raw red oak.

To cold light I wake
empty of what I was;
and sure of nothing
but windows and oaks,
and contented almost

to be contented
in contemplation
of oriental perspective—
the higher up each pane
the deeper the wood,

patches of snow becoming
patches of white sky—
I meditate upon
such distinctions
and indistinctions.

Three Birds in One Cypress

In a glimpse of its flying, its deep-mouth pouch,
I say pelican, but no, when it lands in the top
of the cypress, its blue-gray wings fold with grace.
A pelican never settles his elbows any way but
awkwardly. Now through binoculars, the pouch
stretches out, a neck curves up to an elegant
crown, a slip of black feather like a fashionable hat,
straight javelin beak, and directly in line with the beak
a sharp yellow eye, a brow etched like wood grains
around a small knot. A heron, I know him. A Great Blue.

I've seen a vulture in the same tree and, yes,
there he is, brown and black hunched down in his nasty
feathers. His naked ugly wrinkled red head, I admit,
always a pleasure to note. In sweeping the lens
to his perch, I catch yellow, then focus: a beautiful bird,
black-and-white wing stripes easy to see even when worn
like a herringbone coat, and that gold head and breast.
A hawk, for sure. I search through Peterson's
but can't find him. I know Diane will know
straightaway: Juvenile Northern Harrier.

Now in the gray light of early evening, a sailboat
is making its way to the harbor. Tacking north
and east into wind, it comes closer and closer,
past the island of noisy cormorants and seals.
A fog has settled over the headland. I know
I'm not there, or there where I'd been only
yesterday looking for whales, their spouts far out
but visibly there. I walked the footpaths, tried

to name the flowers. But here, here I am
looking through these wide, open windows,

finding words and names for what I can see,
looking for a glimpse of the self in ignoring it,
putting it on the other side of binoculars, making it
small, letting it drift, go to seed or to silt,
catch a current of air and be blown out to the sea,
high with a gull's view, waiting for, no, glutting after
what the tourists have left me, needing a gyroscope.
Safe-alone in Dick's house I could choose which bird
to look at, as long as he lasted. I chose the yellow
of the Harrier, as still as an owl until he flew.

Sleeping and Waking

I hear cars on the highway as I fall asleep,
and a foghorn in the harbor—not the bell buoy
I remember and wish for—an electronic pulse
every fifteen or twenty seconds, and beyond,
the silent presence of the sea. Thoughts
and corrections of thought, feelings refining. What changes
at morning is light and more cars, the foghorn
a constant, and the dark massive headland.
Thinking begins in the window: a creek through marshes,
cypresses. On dry flats in the distance white birds
pick through mud for what the tide has left them.
Narrative happens, fiction, and lyric cry,
the wheeling and tilting of three vultures, fingers
on their wingtips feeling the air, and what the crabs do.

Starfish at Pescadero

1

I thought I wanted an Eastern mind,
a void emptied out of meaning and sequence and emphasis,
but this river coming down for miles from the mountains
never empties entirely into the sea.
We are walking toward—what I don't know,
something you want me to see.

An egret wades the reedy edges.
His yellow eye peers a long time at a shadow.
I'm fishing too, casting lines
how far into knowing?
We cannot keep as we are.

I want, I think, to be one of the fishermen,
leaving as we arrive. They are carrying out a long boat,
a thing of craft and labor, seams and joints perfectly fitted,
smoothed out and sealed up in amber coats of varnish,
the blond wood gleaming gold.

In a dream of a time when I was barely awake,
I have heard them stealthy in black light before dawn,
stirring the current, whispering, sounds that carry over water:
boat knock, fish rise.

To want and to want and not to have.

Water winks a widening ring. A marsh hawk
wheels over us—the white patch on its back

unmistakable—head up, heavy wings beating.
Has it noticed white cloud as it rises and rises?
The ocean's not far, just over the dunes. It breathes
like a shell. Everything I know is tidal, temporary.
If this is the day. If this is the last day.
Will I ever want to know what I want to say?

Soft, soft, our footfall. Everything is so far: my camera
at the root of the tree where I left it, and you,
walking ahead of me, silent and still as a pond,
into which everything sinks.

2

Cliffs and coves are also gold, sandstone shaped
by oceanic motion. Tides and storms
carve the heaviest spaces of earth.
Rock shifts, sanddrifts mound or cave into
new rock pools, sea anemones open and close,
all life undulates fragility.

You find unfastened a purple-red starfish
washing in the tidal slip and lift it up for me.
Ink-red patterns in relief on its spiny back,
hieroglyphs, ancient inscriptions I decipher—
    lambda, lambda, lambda—
strings of Greek syllables I would sing for you
in an optative mood.

3

I have not loved you in all seasons, only this one,
summer turning gold into autumn

and the California coast stretches long as usual in a mist,
longer in a bright day like this one, water unfurling
like silk along chalk cliffs, sky and sea lapis,
a white edge curled farther North like fur.
Every line in the landscape is hard with clarity
and whatever this is
is hard with clarity.

Teach me. Tell me. I am listening
like a morning bird of the marshes
hidden among dry brown grasses.

You cannot see me loving you.

4

Several miles up San Gregorio Road
the strawberry man can't read your T-shirt:
Fly fishing on the Rogue, you say.
                              Wild fishing, he says.
He counts coins in your hand,
his own hands small, root-gnarled, pig-knuckled.
We exchange looks as we walk
                              from the tin shed into
blue-big sky. Your hands dribble water from a green bottle
to clean the berries.
                    He's watching us,
a scruple in his eye, a baffled or knowing
wonderment. I can't say which.

By the sea again, heading south toward Pescadero,
I pass you a large red bead of a berry by the stem.
Stem and all, all at once
                    you take it in your mouth

from my fingers. I don't know if I know what I mean
or if you do.
                   In a fog of yellow dust, I see again
the farm-grimed fingers of the knot-tight little man who,
from the grease-black engine of his truck,
looked up and touched
                              the tip of his hat.

5

I'm being silly on our walk up the beach.
A dry stalk of kelp my baseball bat, and here's a baseball,
one flap undone, wet and wobbly in white air,
and a light bulb from a yacht offshore brassy in my mouth.

You take a photograph of me, with bulb, with ball, with bat,
ready to strike. Me on the beach at Pescadero,
I'm throwing the ball up for your photograph
to remember me.

6

I kneel by a tidal pool to unfasten a starfish,
points curled round the ragged end of black rock.
I claw at its edges. Water ripples light
around my cold fingers, prying the starfish,
Nothing loosens. The nail rips.

I suck thin blood clean from the wound
and see the starfish in my watery shadow,
its purple-red like the purple-red of our starfish,

but alive with a wild tenacity. It won't let go
and will not float like the dead into my hand.

We will come again, you say, to Pescadero
and colors of the sea will be different,
new animals in old rock pools, seawinds pushing our hair.

Something like knowledge washes over us like a wave.

The Whale

Somewhere out there you are walking; maybe you've gotten
as far as the beach and taken off your shoes or pulled
binoculars from your pack to see a bird better, or a boat,
or the island of seals. And you've wondered by now, as I do,
will they be there forever, the beach, the birds, the seals,
figures, you among them, dear friend, of this landscape
I see from my window, a frame on a changeable weather,
everything, not just the tide, in flux, faraway but soon.

And what if you've paddled your kayak into big winds
beyond easy waves of the harbor? What if you've taken on
sea chop, its wild unknowable currents and swells?
A whale cruising for krill might graze your hull,
tip it. What I honor is your brave imagination, not that
you play it safe: you know you don't know what's possible.

Glaciers

Alaska

We had a picnic by the glacier, its shear wall
close on the other side of the narrow river.
Just looking at its face made us colder.
Its ice not smooth, tall dribbled peaks,
frozen stalagmites, white with veins
of dirty gray and streaks of cobalt blue
like milky opals. We heard it crack and calve,
a large chunk crashing in the water
the size of a small car. We waited for another
as we ate sandwiches, sipped tea, dug
our fingers in a bag of trail mix, as if watching
a movie, ice melting, plot thickening.
I felt unsteady on an earth of cataclysmic
changes. Big things should make us feel secure,
rocks solid and forever, mountains immovable.
Here a certain observable rearranging,
the glacier inching north, receding. Strange,
so little reckoning. Bald eagles in tall pines
hunched down in their shoulders looked exactly
as I felt, enervated, fiercely observant
yet stumped, frozen, waiting to be changed.

New Zealand

I hiked the Rob Roy track along the loud
cold river. Ten kilometers there and back.
It was an easy hike, some altitude gain,

some patches of mud, the usual roots and rocks,
boulders and fallen trees to go around
or climb over. A green November spring,
trees dripping fog and mist, and then it cleared
and just ahead and up and up there it was,
the Rob Roy glacier, the massive white
glare of it. We lay around on warm rocks
and watched for sprays of ice before we heard
the booms. Something huge broken off, racing
like a skier, bumping, tumbling, plunging
to the bottom. How majesty stuns! I said
it was the most beautiful place I'd ever been.
I can't remember well enough to say so now.

Perhaps

Early fall, Orion is rising. I walk my dogs
up the street. Houses on either side are full
of the latest generation. Lulls and whispers.
It's frightening to think how long it has taken
to arrive here. The idea of vastness is a fastness.
All those stories of creation shape and contain.
What we shuffle through has no terminals or edges.
Geometry is comfortable and so is physics,
the flashlight I carry, the watch I wear.
Suddenly my pups strain against their leashes;
they want desperately to pursue something quick
in the dark. Scent of coyote. Scent of deer.
Perhaps an ordinary red-eyed raccoon.
Our little minds. Beautiful fictions.

Two

Doubtful Sound

A little before Noon we passed a little Narrow opening in the land,
where there appear'd to be a very Snug Harbour.

—Captain James Cook's Journal of his First Voyage
Wednesday, March 14, 1770

He had come to a place he knew
he should not go into. Sounded
and had no ground with 70 fathoms Line.
Latitude 45 degrees 13 minutes South,
by his own observation. Windless, a sudden slack
in the sails, all cranks stopped, a soundless
drifting in calm waters, through mist,
by waterfalls, rock and tree islands.

Inland behind this opening were Mountains,
their summits Cover'd with new Snow,
and no wonder the air that morning so cold,
the land on either side of this Harbour rising
a very considerable height, almost perpendicular from the Sea.

He saw clearly no winds could blow there
but what was right in or right out,
that is, Westerly or Easterly, and certainly
it would have been highly imprudent
to put into a place that his ship could not have got out of
but with a wind he'd found to blow but one day in a month.
Some of his seamen wanted him to harbour at any rate,
without in the least Considering
either the present or future Consequences.

He was a man not of temptations but of measures,
exact locations on the chart he charted. He knew winds
to be fickle and men to have passions and instincts—

for fresh food and adventure, for now and again the assurance
of solid ground, some time and space apart.

He trusted his instruments and tables, the fixed stars,
when he could see them and mark them. On his chart
he named this opening Doubtful Harbour,
and drew it as a shallow indentation in the coastline,
not knowing how far or how deep it cut into and divided
the high mountains, not knowing it was a sound
of remarkable beauty, a Siren's song.

On the Way to Keats' House

Three olive-skinned girls appeared out of nowhere
chattering a musical staccato like birdsong
or chant or machine gun, their fired syllables
a perfectly articulated Italian.

It happened of course suddenly on a street
near the Spanish Steps. One had her hand
on your hand on your purse. Another thrust
a paper she hoped you would look at

under your nose. A third slipped between us,
liquid-black eyes up in my face, pleading,
attempting to draw me away—the posture
of supplication except she was so close.

Their arms richly sunned, their hands floating.
Sisters maybe, of assorted ages, nine to twelve.
Pretty colored dresses and ribbons.
Clever operation except adolescents

don't scare us. We could read them like books.
So you kept your hand on your purse, and I
without thinking, brought up, right under
a chin, my stiff plastic map of Rome.

I grunted: "Non" and they fled like swallows
around a corner. They could have been
running off to play hopscotch at recess,
sly scholars of randomness and surprise.

I'd like to have seen them in my classroom,
hunched over smudged errors in their homework,
parsing the grammar of a sinuous sentence,
or reading something cold and crafty in English.

They could have taught me something:
legerdemain, how to sleep in a crate, sort
bottles, find a soup bone, spot the well-off
and the well-to-do, the easy pockets.

I'd learn to steal. And then steal the secret
elixir: one more day, one more breath,
one more flight above penury. Keats died
in a room in a rented house by the Spanish Steps.

He breathed this bright air and imagined cold
stubble to be warm, as some pictures are warm.
His feverous mutter of lines he knew by heart:
Blow wind and crack your cheeks — and to no one

in particular, to the ceiling, to the plaster
roses on the ceiling: *And my poor fool is hanged.*
The girls fled like swallows around the corner.
I was hungry, hollow, mean, frivolous.

Colossus

At noon we climb the Palatine, a day so hot we do
what we can to forget heat blooming in our bodies.

You don't want to be here. Your skirt sweeps
the tall parched grass as you move over the hill,

picking a way through marble rubble. What you want
is a place in the shade of cypresses and a view again

of the rose we saw this morning, a single thorny cane
winding up the one standing column in the Forum,

red blossoms at the top of fluted stone. In such heat
the mind seeks relief from every present moment—those lions

in the Coliseum, their bloody mouths suddenly vivid to me.
I take an odd pity on them, goaded and hungry, ready to devour

any manacled Christian thrown in their way. We prowl the hot
red sand of the hill as though we are stalking something.

Some fragments of inscriptions I try to read but the Latin
is broken. We have no language for anything we feel,

stumbling through a field of big blocks tumbled, column
drums scattered like joints of a giant's backbone.

A shoulder moves, a head turns. Everything changes
when you see the toe of the Colossus and set your small foot

next to it, large and exquisitely carved, the flesh scrolled
into edges of the polished nail—all that remains

of the human aspiration for form, the rage to destroy
whatever is larger than himself. Who could understand these things?

We are so puny among the fragments of the gods, our appetites
mean, our imaginations shrunk and dimmed, belief bled out

of us long ago. What I want in all this heat and history is simply
something to eat, to find a shade away from the glare of white stones.

I look through my camera at the toes. You rub the leather
of your sandal against the stone and laugh and laugh.

Fireworks

Maybe it's from the *stadio*, I said, looking out
beyond Fiesole at the fireworks. It's so close,
you said, as we heard again, as we felt

another thick puff of rocket. We could see it
streaking up the night sky, then exploding
white light like milkweed blooming

in time-lapse photography, quickly bigger
and bigger until its geometry collapsed,
all its little flares curling into delicate parabolas,

arcing like weeping limbs of a crystal willow.
And that was your favorite. I liked the pure Italian,
three green stars shooting up and unfolding like neon

sea anemones floating loose in watery night.
When we thought it was over, black-green centers
softly pulsed open, red spots glowed like Mars.

We stood on the terrace and watched.
What are they celebrating? we wondered,
neither of us wanting to move to find a travel book.

Ten, maybe fifteen minutes, when the show was over,
you walked inside and closed the screens just right.
My arms grew cold on the marble tabletop.

Your light went out. The sky clear and dark.
The sweet-burn of powder came to me and thousands
of stars consuming their fiery heart-cores.

The Magpie

At 2 am, he kills himself in his truck.
After beer with his buddies, watching
NCAA basketball on a screen above the bar.
His wife gone to bed at home, his two sons
asleep in their tiny beds, he's too awake
to settle down, so he drives country roads,
gas tank loaded, fast in the middle of nowhere.
A hard swerve from a rut. Solid old pine.
Everything turns over and catches fire.
Shotgun shells go off in the flatbed.
Dental films confirm. My sister's first son.
Not much to bury. He's thirty-five.

On the phone—furies of a ripped-out mind.
Metal, plastic crumpled, cracked.
Burnt oil, rubber. Flesh, bone. Ash.
Shell shock. She's already been
to the scene. The gash in the tree.
Why? why? why?—tumble
over and over. How it happened.
Quarrels with his wife. Early morning
coffee with his father at his father's
kitchen counter. After night shifts,
he doesn't go home. She blames
the wife. Has already told
her grandsons: Daddy was killed;
he won't come back in his truck.

On the day of my nephew's death,
I'm in Paris, an apartment in Montmartre.

A pair of magpies are building a nest
in a treetop level with my window.
Each after the other flies in with long
clean sticks, tufts of fiberglass
insulation from a construction site,
styrofoam, gumwrapper glitter.
The tree is beginning to leaf out.

Day after day I visit paintings:
Monet's *The Magpie* at Musée d'Orsay.
Small, still bird on a gate rail in a wintery
landscape, bare trees heavy with white ice.
The barn and sky pale, pale yellows.
Hint of blue in shadows on snow.
Day after day I witness what doesn't matter
much at all, what repeats and flies away,
the tolling of the bells of Sacré-Cœur.

April in Paris

In the Tuileries' round pond, the fountain spray
is a mist in the windy sky. It's April. It's Paris.
Trees are ready to blossom or leaf out,
tulips on tall stems are fat and tight,
arcs of forsythia already blaze.
There's nothing to do but watch a piece of the world
which is not the world. It's all so beautiful here.

Around the pond children wield long sticks
to push wooden boats from side to side.
Girls and boys run to be ready before
boats knock—they rush to be deft,
to touch tenderly. There's no anxiety here:
the simple glee of learning what's predictable
and what's not, vagaries of wind in the sails
as the boats race or veer or tangle or tip,
but the wind sorts them out.

Nearby in a stall, an old man makes the boats
and rents them out. He is rigging a sail, a blue one
on a red boat. There are green boats and yellow
boats and purple boats too, and the colors of sails
are one color or two or patched many colors.
Children's jackets are the same colors, and their shoes
laced with strings they have just learned to tie.
Parents, having found a thing to do that's easy,
that makes everyone happy, relax on benches
around the pond and watch the children.
There's a kind of settling down here, a balance.

I don't envy the children or their parents
or even the old man, though perhaps I should.
A kind of miracle these boats, their solid hulls,
and canvas geometry, the mechanism of rudders.
Behind him on a shelf, some masts are broken,
sails in tatters, rudders splintered off. It's chancy
out here in the weather, and day after day
he takes chances and gives pleasure to the world.

I'm sitting in a state of mild despair,
as if swirled up high above a circus looking down
from a drift of cloud over the center of Paris—
I know it should be enough to love the world.
I feel nothing, or so little.
I watch a boy push a boat with his stick,
a confident red boat with a red sail, that takes
what the wind gives and does what it can.

Boats

In the basement of the Doge's Palace we drink coffees
and watch boats go by in the window
which is really a door with steps
sinking down in the water.

It's morning, the sun just high enough to shine
on water glimmering emerald, glimmering amethyst—
lapping the stone walls of houses along the canal,
lapping the green stone steps going down
to the water in the doorway.

Quietly and carefully for days, we've been quarreling.
Our talk is about maps and directions,
where to eat, what museums we want to see.
We nod to each other politely like nuns in an abbey
where the rule is silence, where piety is so sickeningly good
one is constantly out-gracing the other.
No one is keeping score, but we're developing
habits of disengagement:
every morning we find a place for coffee;
every night you read a book;
we have no conversations about art.

The glass around the doorway is arranged in panels like a prism.
From the right, from the left, we can see a boat coming slowly
before it passes before us. The narrow canal
thinks it's a river always flowing
under the Bridge of Sighs to the sea.

Everything in Venice is colored intensely.
Cases of *aqua minerale* stacked high on a freight boat

are bright orange and blue, the bottles themselves
shipped in for tourists are bright blue.
Freight boats are orange or red or green.
Everything in each boat is one color, the seats, the oars,
the metal fittings, the outboard motor, if it has one.
A long freighter now sliding by is a garish cobalt blue,
another coming after is a sick parrot green.
I am sick myself this morning, sick
with a green sickness of the silences, the uneasy civilities.

A blue boat of red *pomodori* is coming under the Bridge.
Left and right I see it from all sides in panels like planes
in a Cubist painting, colors and shapes colliding, round reds
spilling over the squares of wood boxes. In clusters they hang
on green tangles of vine. And lettuces and *melanzoni* in open boxes
are tumbling over each other, purple and green,
fresh, remarkably fresh in the fetid air
and so close to the foul, beautiful water.

The boatmen are unfailingly courteous to each other.
They read a language of gestures, a code
steeped in tradition, a version of horseman's dressage,
their boats just grazing each other.

Sometimes with the slow grace of a dancer, an oarsman
touches a foot to a wall, lightly pushing away,
adjusting the course, holding a balanced leg high.
An ancient agility I admire in the blood of Venetians.

And contrary to what you might see in a book
or imagine: gondoliers are not all slim, neatly pressed
in black-and-white stripes and white sailor collars.
They do not all sing arias.

I see one coming in the glass, arm steady up on his oar,
feet set on a length of red patterned carpet

on the black polished deck of his gondola.
It drifts for the moment in the crowded canal.

Boat knock.

Boats are unloading. The gondolier waits his turn
to thread a way through congestion. His shoulders arched
muscular and full, he is thick in the middle like Falstaff
and already sweating, his olive face ruddy.
His white shirt sticks. He's hatless.
His gondola is empty, the nose of its shining,
big silver key coming now in the doorway.

I see him and wonder how you see him
and wonder too what you've been thinking,
drinking your coffee, seething in your own humidity
and desire for someone handsome, who sings arias.

Slowly, slowly, I'm thinking,
the whole palace is sinking
and the green stones of the green steps
with the green undulating tongues of slime
are crumbling with rot.

Horse at Murano

You left the hot room of the glass furnace,
heat out of thick heat, humid,
unbearable, unbreathable

and so missed the muscular
brown sweating man who
from the red glob of glass

pulled the shape of a horse,
the head, each leg, the tail.
I was surprised

there was so little blowing in the long pipe.
He'd turn his head to reach it
like a flutist, briefly.

Mostly he took advantages of gravity,
a few spare moves, deftly
lifting and dropping and turning

the flowing glass. It took him
less than a minute for detail of eye,
of mane, of fetlock.

I was surprised he wore no gloves.
surprised that the glass cooled so quickly.
He set him up on the table for the tourists.

Meanwhile you had found a tree
by the water and sat in a hot shade
looking your beautiful self,

though somewhere down, deeply
contained and composing,
you were furious

with me for something I'd done or
not done or said, whatever —
that we'd ended up here

in Murano by the hot sea
from which matterless matter
I spin this.

Birthday Sonnets

1

A book of Heaney for breakfast on my birthday,
new poems from places I've been to, the day-dry
heat of Parnassus, frieze of the Augean stables,
Heracles broken and hurting. I remember
Nestor's sandy Pylos, his excavated palace
and tally of goats. I sipped ouzo on a terrace
with a gull's view of the harbor, the empty masts
of black ships, a blood sky darkening the islands—
glares and flickers we live in, colors of Homer.
Love poems disguised as quarrels or quarrels disguised
as love poems.
      In Connemara, after the birds had flown,
she was glad they'd stopped in the car; her hand turning
the key trembled. Lines steady themselves on paper,
sonnets shape words into losses, quickenings.

2

She arrives in a small box of cotton in blue
figured paper from Florence, rows of tiny
mirror birds facing each other, beaks
not touching, the pattern repeated all over.
Inside, a blue-on-white shard of a Ming bowl
rimmed in silver and set with an eye for a chain.
A few strokes and there in profile: a girl
among reeds, one feather blue line at her back,
one bent in her hand, testing green strength.

I study her round shoulder, the soft sheen
of her porcelain face, the curl of blue reed.
I don't know who she is or for whom she waits
by the blank water, by the rock, if it is a rock,
or another face, like hers, broken off.

Suzhou

1

An old woman wheels two babies in a rickety carriage,
a blanket falling underneath through a torn-flap hole,
one rubber rim loose on its warped wheel, the carriage
meant for one baby, these well fed or poorly fed,
not enough protein, no bones in the faces, small black
eyes embedded in puffed-up flesh, hard to tell their ages,
at least two, maybe older, not crying, unmoving,
yet clearly alive, their mouths gnawing tiny fists.

You want baby. You take. No charge.
The woman rushing forward extends both hands.

I walk over the bridge to the boats, the picturesque
gray-wood structures of shops on the dirty canal,
strings of red lanterns, tables for tourists.
I find carved chopsticks made of rosewood
and a hard-black wood-like ebony but not ebony.
Something authentic for which I pay too much.

2

There were more teachers in the classroom than students,
everyone taking notes, their faces shining as if they'd heard
a strange music—poems singing their own English
as dangerous as meaning. Something happened to them,
to me. Their own language I was developing an ear for,
the almost bending of the body to make the pitches

to say to the children, "Good morning!" ZĂO SHANG HĂO.
I heard it in the night song in the garden, two lovers singing
their longing. A flute over the water in dim light,
its weird floating vibrations came to my skin, and when
at another pavilion a young woman in yellow silk
touched the strings of the long guzheng, its polished
wood gleaming under the sweeping roof of the shelter,
I knew—somewhere soft in my middle, a new place for feeling—
that she knew that the sound of the soul is plaintive,
though it may not speak its truth or say its meaning,
that pain can issue its beauty when the heart is open.

Pigs in the River

Everywhere I went in Shanghai, people were talking
about pigs in the Huangpu River, the number up to 8,000
and growing, 12,000 carcasses fished out of the river
that flows through the city, by the Bund, under the Pearl.
It would not be polite to speak of pigs in the river.
I didn't. I ate chicken, I ate duck, I ate pork
in the finest restaurants in Shanghai.
I thanked my hosts effusively, repeatedly,
learned a few Chinese phrases just to do so.
There were pictures in newspapers, on the web,
young men with long poles pulling bobbling bloated
pigs into boats. Government announcement:
All-out effort. Remove pigs from river. Before they rot.
Foul drinking water. Quality of water still good. Okay.
The regulations of China require the destruction
of pigs infected with virus. What's a farmer to do
but dump sick pigs in the river? Make someone else's problem.

After solitary work of pulling something from nothing,
we artists of the word, the canvas, the keyboard,
take a break from a soul-breaking business.
We've been playing Commie Pong in the evenings
in Colony Hall. The rules of the game are few.
Five six seven players with paddles, bats, rackets—
there's a quibble about terminology, culture, etymology:
ping-pong, wiff-waff—run around the table, manage
somehow or someway to whack the orange ball,
backward and backhand, up to the gallery, against a wall
or a post or bookshelf, through the wicket of a player's knees.
Just hit it. Sometimes, yes, it does happen, it goes over

the net in one bounce and in one bounce is returned.
Good. But not essential. Eyes. Corners. No bunching.
Keep it going. Keep moving. Those are the rules.
I've gotten good at making it someone else's problem.
Then there's the boot rule when play must stop absolutely.

I've thought a lot about sick pigs in China,
about Shanghai, which began as a quaint fishing village.
Conrad loved it. Now the rivers are so polluted, even off shore
nothing is edible. Fish to be eaten is farmed in the provinces.
I saw fields and fields of fish farms on the way to Suzhou.
Everything, it seems, badly managed. On the drive back
to Shanghai, the skyscrapers grew taller and shinier, looming,
multiplying before me: a booming international megalopolis
of commerce and finance, and designer watches. Exports.

Imports. Whenever I've felt superior, disdainful, I've learned
to anticipate the bounce, the ball coming back at me
from an odd unexpected direction,
the awkward choreography, ridiculous poses.
Eventually we cannot suppress laughter—the absurdity
of it—so many dead pigs in the river.

Now let's talk about the planet, the air that we breathe,
the water, its animals, especially the silkworm.
People for the Ethical Treatment of Animals
go ballistic about Number One Silk Factory in Suzhou.
Death of the larva boiled in its cocoon, 30,000 cocoons
to make one beautiful silk blanket. I bought one.

You and I, in America, let's talk about
the developing world, the world we are developing.
Let's talk about the beginning and end of the world, when the ball
hits the boot, there's entropy, and all playing stops.

Photographs, East and West

When I was a tourist, I traveled carelessly,
taking my time designing shots to remove
power lines, telephone wires, and ugly,
upright poles with glass knobs and large metal
canister transformers. They cut across
Tuscan fields of sunflowers and haystacks.
The best photo I have is of gondoliers taking a break,
lying back on the velvet cushions of their gondolas,
arms behind their heads, their funny upturned
ballet shoes pointing at the camera. Flat straw
hats tilt over their faces. Their shoulders ache.
Or they've just been counting money they've made,
their boats pulled together, rope-looped
around blue-and-white barbershop pilings.
I can't make out if they are friends or lovers,
if they're telling stories or jokes on the tourists.
Green water glimmers in the canal, oily irregular shadows.

In Kuala Lumpur, I saw corrugated galvanized
steel sheets fastened crudely together to make huts
for whole families to live in. Smoke rises gray
and thick where women cook, sweet grease in the air.
I took pictures of nature's solid geometry,
red bamboo and green coconuts, and a man
with the brown face of a sage smoking a yellow pipe.
I saw dirty pigeons and greedy monkeys in the Batu caves,
a wonder of the world I wouldn't have missed.
Then, a woman screamed and a burly man on the tour
set his arms akimbo like a linebacker. I admired
his American temerity as he stepped into shadow

and saved her—from robbery or rape, I never knew.
What we edit, we can't understand,
or don't want to. I never took his photograph.
I spent my money on postcards and silk.

Three

Landscape with Groundhog

I have nothing to say about the groundhog, his quick
abstract waddling
         from the gray-weathered barn
toward the water trough meant for the cows.

Faraway and invisible, they browse the slope
near the gray-feathered trees
            by the train tracks.
He lifts his head to sniff the early air, something

foreign in it, as blind almost with ground-darkness,
he knows that I'm here.
              It's March. Tiny water-light
beads slide on his whiskers. Nothing else

moves but a crisp wind in the tips of weeds.
I have nothing to say about
           the engine that pulls
its rumbling load through the valley toward some definite

town. Nothing to say about the murder of crows
in the scratch of trees.
           If they love the sun and white cloud
settled on the sky like a stain, they have not said so.

I have nothing to say about the shadows of fence posts
or the electric wires
           or the rust-tin roof of the sagging
barn. If it is sin to be ignorant or to have nothing to say,

then is it moral to envy the groundhog his ignorance
of the barbed-wire fence he slips easily under,
                              his dark knowledge of an indirect
way toward the infinite field of brown winter grass?

Orca Cannery

All the wrecked rusted objects of the cannery litter
the property, rails and rail trucks, gears and a piece
of gigantic machinery that must have been a pressure-
cooker canner. Rooms for workers converted
for paying guests. Comfortable rooms with large
window-views of the sound: blue-dark wide water,
an island of rock and conifers farther off than it looks.
Kayaks, rainbow colors, are lined up near a small
blue house, full of waders, wellies, paddles.
A faded-red shack at the back of the kitchen,
leaning, dilapidated, was and is a smokehouse;
a funny-fangled elbow of smoke pipe
sticks through the roof. In the hollowed-out cannery
with its sign, 1886, sport fish is gutted,
fileted, vacuum-packed in freeze boxes
for shipping home. Gulls hang around
for toss-outs; tasty bits of salmon on the bone.
Frenzy of wings, screaming appetites.
Docks rotted to poles, some slanted, still,
good perches. As the sun like the tide drifts down,
a bald eagle, common as dirt, returns to watch.

I walk to the corner of the cannery for the show—
gulls fighting over red flesh, fish heads, gray-blue
strings of gut—and see a waterfall pouring out
of a rock-cliff of green undaunted trees. Memory
looms the air: the kayak, the waterfall, the red-mud
river of a broken honeymoon—a durable territory.

History tells of Seward's Folly, languages
of native peoples lost, the Valdez disaster,

the fragility of fisheries, the numbers of canneries closed.
The herring have not returned, not in their old numbers.
Memory is a mathematician, an old fool, a puck.
Beauty's fault is that it recalls disaster.

Fleming Spit

It was a trick and a chance and they took it because
they had to. For them there are no delusions.
For us there is always the illusion of hope.

Let loose from the hatchery some make a run
to the sound, then to the sea, six years to grow fat
with oil, some to be stormed, caught, slit open,

frozen, canned, eaten. Many return but not to spawn.
I caught a king salmon, a big one, early in his turning
to red, still virile, wild on the square of herring

I'd hooked on. Bait and lure. So many lies
we can't see in this chancy world. The meaning
of meaning. Nothing we know can prepare us.

When I set the hook in his lip, he was mad to be free,
shooting arcs all over the pond. Tip of my rod up,
I kept him shallow. Near the end he bent deep again,

seeing the light, the shadow-monster that is me,
the monster that you know shows up near the end
of the story to rip out the gills. Blood on my hands,

dark on the stone like a ruby. A kind of nobility
in not yielding. Backbone. Patience. Endurance.
Some choices we have. Some chance. Some fisherman's luck.

Rockport

1

We've come a long way in the dark to the end of the river.
Light from the lighthouse has swept over us all night,
steady and sexual as a song of love or grief.
Morning in soft fog, we walk all the way out to the lighthouse.
This is the mouth of the bay, the gray sea.
I gather in my pockets blue stones from the rock-quay
and we think both at once of Chaucer's *Breton lai*,
the marvelous good wife, the vow, the black rocks of Brittany.
We believe in the magic and dangers of love, the impossible
possibilities. We know the origins of tales of romance.
The other side of the lighthouse might as well be
the other side of the world. No one can see us
as we look out to the sea, as our hands reach out for each other,
as I touch with cold fingers your small face.

2

We stopped to look back sometimes as we climbed high
and higher above the Rockport light, the nearly noon sun
finally burning through, the whole bay turning a violet blue.
We had never imagined a place more beautiful. Still higher,
another surprise, a chapel cut out of stone, abandoned
or unfinished we never knew. Side-by-side we grew colder,
our hands clasped into fists in our laps to stay warm.
A table that might have been an altar was bare. It seemed
not a place to pray, sounds of the bay were too far.
We had no language for what we had gone into.

Who understood what it was, if anyone?
And who first heard the whir of wings or saw
the bright songless throat of the hummingbird
trapped high in a corner, buzzing and bumping like a fly?

Cape Dunes

*. . . you might have seen our tracks in the sand, still fresh, and
reaching all the way from the Nauset lights to Race Point,
some thirty miles,—for at every step we made an impression
on the Cape, though we were not aware of it, and though our
account may have made no impression on your minds.*

—H. D. Thoreau
Cape Cod, 1855

What Henry Thoreau came to see we survey
from a modern tower in a public park.
An arrow points sternly like a compass to a place far out
where ships broke up on shoals and black, storm-washed
timbers emerge on certain eroding tides. We look out
and see nothing but the long line of the level horizon,
the sea, and all around us the cape dunes.

It's beginning to rain and sudden fog from the August sea
climbs the long dunes as though it knows
how to move over this landscape, as though it knows
how to overwhelm their sharp intentions.
Their windswept clarity blurs. Low brush and shrub oaks,
hieroglyphs bent together in one curve toward the continent.
A quick wind changes the air we breathe. It's fog I feel.

We try the dory on the sand, pull against the oarlocks
and imagine ourselves the fisherman in Homer's painting,
angled against the horizon—the high surf glazing
his oilskins, his hat dripping, a weird, indifferent
light on his face as he looks back, as he tries to beat
the storm to the harbor—adrenaline like salt in his blood,
like the blood of the gill on his hands, the smell of fresh fish,

its scales shining in the dory like a flash of storm on the water.
We imagine ourselves to be that purposeful.

Some might notice the lines in our faces, gray in our hair
and seeing us walk across dunes, sunk to our knees,
say we move together like characters in a legend
searching for a lost son, an unmarked tree.
Yet your face is luminous in cape light
and when Atlantic wind pushes your hair
from your temples, one might look at you and say,
you were never more beautiful.

Someday we will come back and rent bicycles in the park
and ride the dunes like dolphins, following bike paths
like sensual animals in perfect weather—free like Thoreau
to walk the sand and taste salt-air, to find the tree where he hid
to contemplate the storm, and read what any landscape
can tell us of ourselves in any kind of weather.

Flags

A meadow, a pond, a cedar house set on a knoll,
steep-pitched gables and glass. A 20-acre spread,
or thereabouts, of horse property all fenced-in.
Serious acreage, a realtor would say, a landscape
to die for. And beyond, a pristine forest
of pines, the folding mountains of the rocky north.

One June day when I drove by, on every fence post
an American flag, hundreds of waving, glary
flaps of color. And a four-by-five plywood sign
spray-painted white, blue letters stenciled on.
    IN LOVING MEMORY OF
    PVT. ROY DALE KLEIN
    KILLED IN KOREA 1952
    WERE HIS & OTHERS
      SACRIFICES
      MADE IN VAIN
I recognized, of course, the politics, the question
not-a-question, a still-raw public keening,
as if after all these years someone could
do something. It's 2016, for Christ's sake.
Good soldiers go soldiering on in ambiguous wars.

Sometimes what I resist is what I know
I should embrace, or at least think about.
The guilty pleasure I take in architecture in its place.
My fascination with clamor and debate.
What drives men to the grit and gut of hollering,
to governed aggression, even death, except
constituted meaning, the freedom to possess

life, liberty, the pursuit of happiness —
to put what you mean in words and drag them out.

My own irritable reachings after.
I drew conclusions. The sign was ugly, awful.
I drove on down the bumpy dusty road,
the grand house in the rearview
and the beauty of the horses.

Next time, I stopped and wrote it down
on the back of an empty envelope and saw
close-up what I hadn't seen just driving by,
a pair of jars wired to the corners of the sign,
in each a handful of wilted flowers.

I should have marked it, I cannot be exact.
Somewhere along Colorado County Road 502,
a near-thought like a shooting star crossed
through my shoulders.
                        I was trying to see it
as they saw it, as I drove away from the sign
and the memory of the sign and all those flags.

From every window they'd have a view of horses,
their sculptural shapes groomed and shining,
a light hoof lifted, dropped occasionally,
their soft mouths nibbling meadow grass.

Singing Line

A whole village given to fishing, and I wish
my father were here fishing his broken heart out,
chuckle in his throat when he'd try the new trick,
chunk of herring soaked in red food coloring,
and a fish takes it right away, hooked good
and he already knowing it's a big leaping thing
to coax to the shore, giving him line, playing
him, tiring him out. Seeing me now fighting
a king, big show-off of jumps and runs, drawing
a tight singing line, I like that singing even better
than Sophie Tucker, he would say, loving the crazed
catch of the moment, the line my own line,
the fish my own fish, directly I feel the electric
liveliness of my iridescent silver-rose.

Alpine Lake

The first time I went skinny-dipping,
it was an Alpine Lake, no more than a pond.
We'd been hiking, climbing. The path was steep.
On the map the trail ended at a lake. There was drought

and the dust of drought, red needles in the dying trees.
I was tired of the heat. You ran ahead of me, up
and back, giving me time, not at all fazed.
Drink water, you said. I was doing fine, you said.

There it was: what we wanted to get to, the lake
a lapis stone, a sky-mirror. You were stripping,
daring me, shaming me. *Never!* you said, *Never?*
And strode in and dove. Naked as a hatchling,

awkward, incapable, I folded my clothes
on a fallen tree, under-things under my T-shirt,
without shoes my feet picked tenderly through sticks,
roots, needles, my toes testing bottom — rough,

irregular with sharp slimy-slick stones. I tried slipping
slowly down in the cold. Cold. So cold I abandoned
all modesty, dropped my crisscross arms from my breasts —
I needed balance, hands to catch what I thought

inevitable, my fall. I crouched and pushed out in the ice
of the water where you already so confidently had gone,
your head now and then bobbing up like a turtle.
So much warmer, you said across the lake, with all

of your body down under, even your eyes and your nose.
My dear, so young you could be my daughter, you shamed
me naked. I came up, clean and shivering to see you
grinning in the Sierra summer high lake cold.

Prairie Installation

for Andrea Lilienthal

> *But reading Darwin, one admires the beautiful solid
> case built up out of his endless heroic observations,
> almost unconscious or automatic—and then comes a
> sudden relaxation, a forgetful phrase, and one feels the
> strangeness of his undertaking, sees the lonely young
> man, his eyes fixed on facts and minute details, sinking
> or sliding giddily off into the unknown. What one seems
> to want in art, in experiencing it, is the same thing that
> is necessary for its creation, a self-forgetful, perfectly
> useless concentration.*
> —Elizabeth Bishop

Perfectly useless, yes, I'd say,
those neon paints on prairie cattails.
At first I didn't notice the orange
tips, so tiny gaudy. But slashes
of green on slanted broken blades,
those would catch any eye. Did I ever
see the yellows? I must go back
and look and look. Blown cattails
the least of it, the tips, the blades—
subtle, but shocking—and colors, yes,
as colors! For sure, I'd say, a triumph,
natural impossibles *sliding us giddily
off into the unknown,* into which
Andy had taken us, her eye steady
on what she's done. And we?
We were inarticulate. And then
the four of us walked the prairie
to its end, seeing three yellow
finches along the way. Stopped still,
and heard a concert of high bright
voices, sweet complexities,

and saw the pussy willow canes
two had settled on, the third
perched on a little dead tree.
Then into the woods we walked
and crossed a swinging bridge. Like girls
we played, what fun! and saw the barks
of trees, the elm's gray vertical
diagonals, easily recognizable,
another's rusty shingle-shakes,
a rarity, whose name we didn't know.
Some early flowers blooming in mud,
and tragedies from years of storms,
some glorious rot with lichen plates,
and roots of trees blown over,
and there a monster vine had thickened
round a tree and died with it.
We saw a snake, a toad. I picked
him up, predictably he peed.
And then, three elms grown tall
together, or was it one enormous,
triple-trunked, majestic tree?
Not an introspective day,
the four of us, not much to say—
all of an age to have worked things out,
or not, our lives behind us different
stories, now so far away,
or really unusually concentrated.
Those painted tips like matches struck,
and in that light we had so much
to see. I must go back before
the rains wash all the colors away.

Rim

I wake to light struck green on the far side
of the canyon, everything fresh and wild
with heat. Coyotes nip and yelp like shrill birds
scrabbling over carrion. They have bitten to the heart.
In the aftermath of the kill, I listen to flinty steps
of a doe browsing for shoots between rocks.
Roots dig the wet bottom, buckeyes
bloom defiantly, making fingers, fists.
I've been figuring geometry in my head,
how to build a fence down the slope of the canyon.
My saw, my level, my square, my hammer, my sack
of nails, the posthole diggers—to impose an order,
mechanical and human. I try not to think about
the stack of red heartwood waiting in the garden.

Four

Colman's Well

in memoriam, Michael Miller

All rituals are strange customs of the desperate,
the hard look for meaning, symbols made
of ordinary objects, gestures to grace them.
Consider modern strips of cloth hung in trees
by Colman's well, colors in touch with the body
of someone sick or dying, the dearly beloved's
sleeve carried in a pocket up the raw rock slope
to the spring that runs through mossed-over stones,
ferns flourishing big as trees. Flannel rags
of cotton, wool, polyester—the trashed-up
forest a desecration of the Holy Well.
A dirty hand dipped and hung each clootie.
A persistent belief in a healing holiness Colman
would have wept to see, knowing all suffer and die.

We've walked a short way up from the road
in new boots and rain jackets. Hard to pick a way
through vines running everywhere on big stones,
wet mist dripping from leaf and stone lip,
mouth of rock. Ordinarily impossible to find
this tangled place, Colman's cave and well,
the oratory he built before Rome imposed
strict rule and order for monastic life.
Here wildness itself claims and reclaims
body and earth, green breath in a bewildering
wilderness. Colman wrapped himself
in deerskins to keep warm, trimmed wild beauty
to animal essentials. A worried way to solitude,
the hermit-monk's discipline to let be.

Here under an eagles' eyrie in the burren
with his mouse to nibble him awake, his fly to mark
his last-read word, his rooster to remind him of time,
Colman prayed, chanted Celtic syllables, meditated
in the morning and followed the evening flight of eagles.
A wall remains, an arch. We settle behind it
in the shade and summon his name. Any word spoken
is resonant. Cameras stop whirring and clicking.
Michael, whose idea it was to bring us to
this place, reads his poem about Saint Colman,
who denied himself all comforts except words,
their warm precision flowing from his mouth.
We've trudged up the king's clattering Road of Dishes,
hardly aware of our noise and desolation.

Red Sails

All I can figure, he must have been Irish, the sailor
who sang on our porch after midnight, mother alone
in our house near the Navy Yard, her children sleeping,
my father on the night shift, not home until morning.
Night after night, the sewing machine light
the only light on, her fingers picked stitches.
I remember the stumbling boot on the steps,
the slosh of the bottle, the porch swing creaking,
the rough voice in the same song sung night after night.
　　Red sails in the sunset, way out to the sea —
She'd be still for a moment, then switch off the light
and lie down beside us, listening, listening —
　　Oh carry my loved one safely to me.
I could feel the ferocity of her vigilance.

I didn't know for a long time all the pieces
of the story, the man who left her and went to the war
returned to his other wife in the North. Bigamist,
she told me, his sergeant rank stripped to buck private.
Somehow he survived the Battle of the Bulge
but never came home to my mother and his infant daughter.
　　Red sails in the sunset, way out to the sea —
Now that I've been to Ireland and seen them,
some bright blood-red, some faded, puffed full
in an easy bay wind of a Galway gloaming,
that rough sea-light on the harbor, the black pitch
hulls of the hookers, I know what the song is about,
the whimper suffered, withheld in the listening.
The name was Irish but I've blanked it out.

Woman Fishing

1

I dream a woman with silver hair fishing
an Irish morning lake; her slim canoe
cuts milk-opalescent skim of sky.
One arm stirs craters and vortices.
The paddle never lifts. The image moves
like a short film-clip of vanishing desires.
A red fin rises and rolls in the reedy edges.
Line whips and thrums, its formal elegance
drawn out to the last s-shaped uncurling
of the fly, the deep easy bend of the rod,
sweet play of the run, circling swerves,
the hand a simple slip in the gill, the lift.
I walk to meet her on the shore.
We talk and clean the fish and build a fire.

2

Crystal and silver are set on Irish lace.
The woman with silver hair looks at me
across the table as she listens to conversation
about the war, whether we should or should not
be there. Her husband sits by a peat fire.
Everyone laughs. Their son, on break from school,
talks to me, voluble enthusiasms about
anything Irish. I nod and listen and look at her.
He's a lovely young man who reads Heaney
and Yeats. He knows about curraghs, a hooker's

red sails. He's ferried out to Inishbofin.
He wants me to know what he thinks about
Gretta's secret and Gabriel, Trevor's restraint.
Today he hiked ten miles over the burren.

Above the mantel an eighteenth-century mirror
doubles the room, round sky in silk water.
When I look up, there's a woman with silver hair.

Postmark London

A Hockney swimming pool painting we'd seen at the Tate,
or from the Queen's Gallery that self-portrait
of Reynolds with glasses pushed down on his nose,
better yet, a page from a manuscript in the British Library,
first page of *Mrs. Dalloway*, a spidery purple-ink hand.
I ignored all suggestions for the postcard I would send to you.
My stamp, my pound. You'd said to say hello to Elizabeth.
I found several good ones in her gallery's shop,
photographs of her coronation, trooping the colours,
that keen black-and-white taken by Annie Leibowitz.
I chose a recent one: she's wearing a kerchief, her coat
tweed, blur of trees in the background, a London cold day
or Balmoral, a close-up of that face softly wrinkled
as if she were one of us growing older, looking up, smiling.

Lady Fishing

Not a landscape merely but a woman in a landscape.
She stands almost always by a body of water
lake   river   sea,
            her face in the shadow
of her bonnet, or turned away from the painter
father brother lover,
            whose obsession is
light in the folds of her dress, fabric especially
difficult if white or pale blue and washed out like the sky.

Sometimes the painting is all drapery, skirt lines worked
clean like sculpture
            a ruffle   a ribbon   a furl,
fine brushstrokes figure filigreed edges,
detail of button or lace, gloves pulled high
to the sleeves, wrist covered, rarely a shoe, often
a parasol held open for some picturesque reason.

In Sargent's large painting *Lady Fishing,* his sister
Violet wears the usual flush of white shadows,
her gloves clumsy and useful.
            The lady is fishing,
a subject not appropriate for fashionable exhibition
and so he's painted out the pole she holds,
the length and weight of it in the line
of the shoulder,
            the set of her knee against the front
square of skirt where it breaks and falls triangular.

She seems unaware of the painter. At water's edge
she waits for —
                        you know the little tug —
the fish she imagines circling hither and thither
among blue reflections and green weeds.

Thought has let its line down into the stream
where it sways, minute by minute, letting swells
lift it, sink it until —
                        you know the little tug —
the cautious hauling in and laying it out on grass,
how small, how insignificant this thought,
a fish a good fisherman gives back to the sea.

2

I am thinking now of Virginia scudding out
in a lugger to the lighthouse. She pokes around
among tackle in a wood box on the black deck
fish lines wound tight like colors of threads
on weavers' shuttles
                        yellow   blue   red
colors of old paint too, worn from wood handles
bright and deep in the grain.

Her father stands in the boat reading a book
he's pulled from his coat,
                        its covers mottled blue
like a plover's egg. His mouth shapes syllables
of Greek, the mutter of a phrase he repeats,
as if to let meaning sink in — is that it?
should it be?
                        He looks at a figure on the shore.

Is it blue? Is it green? A woman paints
what he is, the lighthouse over his shoulder.

In the wood box on the black deck, gobbets of fish flesh
have dried gray on orange-rust hooks. Virginia wishes
she had fresh fish bait, a knife to core it out,
the clean smell of fish flesh on her fingers.
She imagines
                    setting anchor in a green swell
or riding boat rock in the purple cliff shadow
over a shipwreck where fish are bedding.
She imagines
                    a fish mouth opening to take
the big hook she's tied on with a figure-eight slip knot,
the line's elegant dip and run, the invisible
dart and cut of the fish
                              she feels in her hands,
the awful muscular course to the surface —
wit against wit, carefully playing it out,
cautiously hauling it in,
                          dab   gurnard
iridescence of scales flashing, deck flop, the red gill
gasping, the slime jaw tight in her fist
so the hook can be pushed back in the throat
swiftly, firmly,
                    the handsome mouth not torn,
the lovely fish alive in her hands.

3

On the 25th of July the weather was fine in Carbis Bay,
swells easy,
                    the fisherman handsome and willing

not to fish. Waiting on the jetty, we tied
new hats on our heads,
                        pushed hemp woof
from an orange sack through gaps in the weave
of the brims,
                        sensual   clever   myopic.

Scudding out in the lugger to the lighthouse,
I wanted to be intent on the present not the past.

   Thought darted and sank
   flashed hither and thither
   setting up such a wash and tumult
   it was impossible to sit still.

I held on to rails of the lugger all the way out
to the lighthouse and thought of Virginia
on the black deck,
                        red stockings in her lap
for the keeper's son. All the way there and all the way
back I thought of fishing, and her not fishing.

Light shone clear through the cleft
in the lighthouse rock. We gave it wide berth, swung out
and back to the harbor.
                        Here and there,
here and there, a zig-zag course from the lighthouse,
my hands and hip pressing the tiller, feeling
swell-force, wind-weight, the wild freedom
of tacking in a head wind.
                        A moment of being,
being there and arriving, coming home
inside a landscape I'd never been to
and finding it true.
                        And then I changed my life.

White Garden, Kent

1 Long Barn

. . . and there I lay in Swansdown and recovered
among brick and brocade, pillows silk from Persia,
you on the stony floor beside me, letting me
tousle your hair, strands of it red-gold
in the English morning sun, bones of my fingers
on the skull of a Sackville.

My dearest donkey West,
As you came in from riding
and stood for a moment in the doorway
at ease in the drape of your trousers,
that aristocratic knee,
you were peeling away your gloves.
I could smell the leather and the stables,
the elkhounds wet from running,
snuffling your boots.

My Dark my Dusky Beauty,
Now at your narrowest table, oak the color
of copper, candles crystal silver set
with two china plates that shine like silver moons,
knees together, we begin the easy flow
of minds going in and out of each other's
without any effort, rhythms like waves, like music
(but not music) by windows glinting black.

Dearest, for whom I would do anything,
I have millions of things to tell you.

Choose for me from steaming pots one tender
piece of—it doesn't matter what, from swirling
browns like Scottish waters from which you fish
a rainbow—one tender piece of eternity.

Kentish Creature,
Unfasten the topmost button of your jersey
and find a squirrel, most inquisitive.
From that platter of fruits on the sideboard,
heaped and tumbling, doubling in mirrors
newly silvered, shadows and planes
and shapes all deliberately disordered
as in a Vanessa or Duncan still life,
feed me sweet seeds of pomegranate
pink-and-orange clustered—your articulate
fingers delicately clawing them loose.
Set them like syllables to burst on my dry tongue.

2 *Sissinghurst*

What we do today—
Go hunting with your hounds. Run
like a fox, curl in the hollow of a tree.
The hounds make music with their mouths tuned
like bells, the shuffle of a snare in dry leaves.
You find a warm green spot, and throw
a whole roast of rare shoulder to the dogs.

What we do today—
Long walk to the butcher in the village.
Luster of pink pearls, silver scales
of fish on ice, the V-notch tail.
You touch the eye for freshness,

a slick black pearl.
A bargain, you whisper.

What we do today—
Picnic in the white garden,
its high brick walls, underplantings
of artemisias, tiny Chinese bells
droop like lanterns. Everything we do
is song without sound, fragrance
of freshly turned dirt,
freesias drunk on cloudy light,
thoughts we come to.

3 *Vita's Sonnet: Rodmell*

Not wanting to withhold anything from each other,
can we end what our bodies do? Salt lip
turns of phrase, purple ink on our tongues.
A ride through the countryside in Harold's car.
He writes fond letters from Teheran about boys
in the office, one with blond hair he throws back
from his forehead. Every word a kind of
faithfulness, and the garden to talk about too,
a vine I need to pull out by the roots.
We know there are dangers, highs and lows
of back and forth visits, the sorrows of our tenderness.
You want too little. Nothing's ever enough.
And there's Leonard on his ladder, pruning his apples.
Leonard, your old brown coat without pockets.

Grasmere

I wanted to steal a boat and row out
and have that feeling of something
looming up. Halfway round the lake
I saw a yellow hull belly up
in the grasses, the wedge end
of a paddle showing just from under,
and a yellow nylon rope loosely coiled,
not fastened or locked to anything.
It would have been easy stealing,
but I didn't stop, or not for long,
a brief imaginary trip
around some islands. My lack
of fervor was a disappointment.
Why was I here if not to take
chances, if not to reach for those
fleeting shivers of another's feelings?

It was the same at Rydal Mount.
A rare morning not packed with
tourists and so I lingered alone
a good while in the poet's room.
Out the window above his desk,
the lake was a distant flat gray pool.
I found I could not feel anything
except the heat of the sun
on the polished wood of his desk
and through the window soft fresh
scents of flowers in the garden.
I whispered lines from *The Prelude*
but heard only a weak voice,
not his, not even my own.

Fresco

We stayed in a monastery cut up into condos, ours with a terrace of dried-up papery roses overlooking Fiesole. The clang of the bell in the morning and evening, the lights of bridges across the Arno, even the road—bumpy, rutted, in places washed out—had its charms. We'd come and go as we pleased, into Florence often, or drive to other hilltowns.

The road to the condo passed by the side of the big priest's house where Sylvia now lived. She gave us the key and showed us how to turn the hot water on, a mystery I never figured out. The trick was to open the faucet even as you put a match to the gas. There was a whoosh and the pilot held. She spoke almost no English, we spoke less Italian, but she managed to answer most of our questions, with nods and laughs and hands flying around her head; enthusiasm was essential, a way to convey good will and patience when no one understood anything.

One of Sylvia's front teeth was missing, the other one oversized and yellow, her pink tongue pressed against it constantly feeling for the missing tooth. Every time we saw her, leaving or returning in our little rental car, she wore the same flower-print dress that fell in folds over her generous middle. She watered geraniums on her porch. She sat on the steps with her knees apart, letting the cool of the shade flow under her skirt.

Farther along, another pair of ruts, hardly a road, cut through a vineyard to a warren of shacks, low to the ground, chickens in the yard. Several vacant-eyed older adults wandered about like children or stood and stared. A hulk of a man with hollow hunched-over shoulders in overalls—no shirt underneath, just the crisscross straps of his baggy overalls—held his tight-knuckled fists under his chin as he dug at the dirt with his heel, kicking the same spot over and over. Several yards away, a thin woman with strands of gray hair falling over her face sucked her fingers, two or three in her mouth, as if from a bottle.

We never talked about what we saw three kilometers from town. We never saw an attendant or any responsible adult, just those standing shadows staring at something on the ground or in the clouds or along the roof of the house—a snake? a shape like a face? a row of rose-breasted doves?—something so fascinating their heads bobbed from side to side as if to the beat of music in their minds.

The thin woman with gray hair falling over her face was usually the closest to the road when we passed in our car, windows up, wheels stirring up dust as we headed down the hill through the narrow streets of Fiesole to the parking garage on the edge of Florence. From there we would walk to galleries and churches. On the last morning—but how could she know?—she looked up and I caught her large smoky eye so oddly cold blank and connected that it held my eye. Her arm lifted as if she were stretching on tiptoe. In the rearview mirror I saw she had turned and was waving good-by.

That summer of indulgence, in fresco colors and hilltowns, a woman sat beside me in our little red car. She couldn't drive a gear-shift; she couldn't read maps. I was happy. Everything was seething with beauty. Sunflower fields and paintings in churches and especially my companion, the woman with the map in her lap. The heat and dust and ache of it, the enigmatic endurance of the silent and inaccessible, like the fringe of ivy under the eave of the eastern gable of the monastery, its root-like sucker-tendrils fastening in the stucco.

Rome Again

I'm trying not to be sleepy on the train
going back to Rome from Florence. We'll see
the Pantheon which was closed and buy that whimsical
pottery in Piazza Navona. Fields of sunflowers
go by, luminous patches, all the brown faces
more of them now as I'm writing,
making up nothing—this is from life.

And more little towns on hilltops with crenellated towers
and cypresses marching ridges like Giacometti soldiers.
In the seat across from me, you move backward
faraway dreaming of handsome Italians, shape
of a jaw, a shoulder, that loose alertness like David
contraposte, his large ready hand.

Winding up and up, the train slips
in a side-to-side rhythm. You lean back
and face the window. Glazed and sealed up
in a sleek Eurocar, distracted by introspection,
meditation on landscape—
                              houses again and streaks
of color, geraniums and trumpet vines pour over
the walls, a family's wash on a line, an irregular
geometry pegged and drying stiff in the heat of stone—
in the belly of motion and time—
                              I consider
the physics of Leonardo's lines that come
to a point in the eye. Here a still moving center
an emptiness where nothing is happening
that has not been happening. Outside, all of Italy

fleeting in your eye, a village's smoldering rubbish
not excluded and yards of rusted-out cars, flattened
and stacked. Patterns of repetition and surprise,
an aesthetic of excess, abundance, abandonment.

In a tunnel, your face is reflected in the shining
black window. Hand to cheek, thumb under chin,
stroke of light on your wrist. I want a metaphysics
for a line in a sketch in a notebook, ink to trace
what is warm but cannot be held, what is
constantly receding. I think of flesh Raffaello
made for the human face among crowds of faces
and elaborate luxuries of Renaissance villas, a window
of Tuscany in the background and the perfectly
painted clothes.
     Clouds over Rome as we approach.
Will it rain? I wonder. We've brought no umbrella.
We are here, you say, as you look through the window,
scanning the anonymous faces in the station.

In the Room the Women Come and Go

No, no, no, she says to her friend with the hat,
it's the soul that's erotic, don't you see?
They crane their necks to the ceiling, looking
oddly like birds, cormorants on pilings.
Maggie stares at the clothes,
the fabrics and colors

furled on the saints, the sleeve of God.
She can't quite see what Mary means.
Not at all. Nothing's nude, she thinks.
Don't you see, Mary says, how they strain
to touch? No, I don't, Maggie says
and drops the topic.

They try to whisper, but their voices carry
across the room. People are moving quietly.
In a corner a woman with white hair is bent
over a magnifying mirror. She focuses
on the face of Isaiah, her fingers delicately
turning a black knob.

How could paint have so much light? she says,
looking up at the stranger who looks down
at the mirror. I'm Anne, she says.
They both look in the mirror.
Yes, it's beautiful, Maggie says,
the transparency

of the sleeve—how did he do it?
Especially—Anne says, looking, looking—think

of trying to imagine the effect from below,
on his back, on a scaffold, close to the ceiling,
like—she almost says it, but won't—
an auto mechanic

wedged under the weight of his car, oil dripping
in his face, the slick of it, intoxicating. Or like
a woman on her back about to receive the weight
of her lover, she's thinking of Cleopatra,
what hurts and is desired, all those
clothes coming off,

going on, Maggie thinks, as Mary,
always technical, opinionated,
walks over to see what they are seeing.
It's controversial about the cleaning,
what came first? the body or the paint
on the body?

evidence of overpainting?
Maggie, who isn't listening, wonders
about the boy he followed through the streets
of Rome to study his curly hair in the sun,
from which he knew what to do
with the head of David,

the singer with his props, not at all cold
like the marble boy in Florence, too white, the sling
too loose in his fingers. Here a face of ruddy shadows,
older, though still a boy, who looks—his hand
in the hair of the giant, his lyre laid by—
a little like her.

She's thinking about the soul of the giant,
how the wind went out of him when his eye

met David's eye. Was it the stone in his head
that brought him to his knees, or enemies close-up
like Achilles and Penthesilea,
they changed their minds?

On the ceiling the fallen giant is still gazing
at the beauty of the boy. There are places in history
when the body itself makes a miracle,
the lover looks and beauty vanquishes
and even the wielding sword of God
is sexual and good.

Yes, yes, yes, Maggie thinks as she moves
to where she can stare up at Daniel,
then Joel, then Jeremiah. They've all assembled
in the painter's mind. Not the flesh. Not the paint.
Mary got it right (here she removes her hat):
it is the soul that is erotic.

She makes a note with a pen and a pad from her purse.
Near the door, she observes faces
in the crowd, oddly assorted clothes
and paraphernalia, jaws and foreheads,
ears, the hair—and the loveliest arms,
none braceleted, some fair.

Light of Troy

We live in the flicker of Troy. Think of gleaming gold,
    what it meant. A siege for justice and beauty
yields carts of collateral damage and treasure.

In the dark, out of breath, up a red slope from the sea,
    a herald carries home a torch from that fire.
News! of the war but his own story too.

The watchman listens and waits, one foot bound
    to the lion gate. He's counted stars, followed
constellations wheeling in yet another summer sky.

The common majesty of boredom. Then torchlight
    obliterates the night and nothing at all is clear.
Fragments and smoke from a city sacked and burning.

When the herald arrives, the watchman won't trade
    truth with his friend. He's simply glad to see him
and listen to his report, blurted, so many details.

His eyes blaze with stratagems of war:
    ten tedious years of brawls, games of assault,
the hunger, the quarrels; then operations of deceit,

word-craft with a chisel-and-hammer plot,
    whispers in the womb of the wooden horse.
The runner perfectly repeats to the Queen

what he's been told: *The city's burnt, sacked!*
    The captain's coming home, in triumph. Unctuously,
the Queen says, *Good, garrulous messenger,*

you've pleased your listener and will be doubly paid.
The promise of gold again. Promotions. Payoffs.
The watchman knows, though an ox is on his tongue,

the net of words woven. There will be no unweaving,
not on his watch. The filth-smeared house is mad.
By the door of the palace, the double ax gleams,

the carpet's clean, rolled out for the victor's
strut. A clatter of iron chains on the road,
and the King arrives in the opulence of power

with his prize, a fuck-crazed girl, burbling
the future in his dirty chariot. The herald
and watchman listen for tricks in the voices.

Come in, says the Queen, tall and clean
in the doorway. Words and gestures toward
intimacies, favors. A cold bath's drawn.

A promise of peace, some beauty that is human.
The lame watchman listens and plays dumb.
The young herald counts his fingers.

Asphodel

I'd never seen asphodel until that long walk above *Kardamili*
a whole field of it on a slope of Tagyetus.
I had to ask what it was,
                    each flower so small
you'd hardly take notice, long stems ribbed weed-like
but a whole field of it, a delicate knee-high plush.
When I walked through—
                    it was all familiar from Homer,
except no one sorted into or out of Elysium,
each of us merely apart and human—
I took the breeze in the asphodel as a sign,
but of what?
            A kind of grandeur running like fire under the skin.
And this is what it is to be mortal, I thought,
and to savor the heat and the dust
that makes the flower pink-tender.

I saw it again under gnarly arms of an olive grove,
near the ruin of a small monastery.
                    No one lived there
but a nightingale on a nest under the eve, her tail lifting
with her heartbeats, a mild panic of intruders.

We did no harm, we moderns, no mumble of prayer
among us to frighten a soul. And no song
from the brooding bird.
                    Just the silent heat
of longing and the faint-sweet of asphodel
flowing up the valley from the sea.

Tomb Paintings

Once I climbed down a ladder into a tomb
in a peach orchard in Macedonia to see
ancient paintings of laurel and pomegranates,
colors of the peach I'd stolen and was about to bite into.
The room cool and so tiny even I bent over,
no sign of human remains. Walls and ceiling
pristine, no peeling paint, no splotches of mold,
a smooth plaster ground for colors washed
in the light of my headlamp, magnified as if by water.
A clean death, I thought, for a woman well-loved,
a delicate, everlasting decorum. Gradually the tomb
filled with gasoline fumes and I climbed up again
to Greek light, a stunning summer heat, and there
the motorcycle man, the owner of the orchard.
The peach in my hand, unbruised, one green leaf.
It's not ripe, he said, it will be hard and bitter.

Tainaron

for H.V.

We'd come to the end of the known world at Tainaron,
the tip of the Peloponnese. A temple
to Poseidon stood here and a statue of the god.
Walls curve up to a round roof,
                              large unhewn rocks
rearranged, the ancient structure later Christianized,
but no icons, no inscriptions.
The god is gone.

A door.
        It was dangerous to walk under
the thick lintel stone.
Inside, light shot through
                         holes between stones.
Shore rocks pocked by acid wind, blood tides, bitter time.
Pebbles with that rhythm of soft grating on the beach.
I'd heard it before in a complaint
                              of "neither" and "nor,"
a song of alarms and confusions—
a black cave nearby, the entrance to Hades.

I saw from the beach a blue and white container ship,
large letters on its side, UNICEF FOOD,
traveling east, making time, passing by this god-
ridden, stark, beautiful place,
                         the end of the known world
where Orpheus lost Eurydice in spite of his song,
and Arion, strumming dithyrambs, came ashore
on the back of a dolphin.

Turbulent music and a kind of cold light.
Cognition. Recognition.
A ruin left alone like many on the Mani.

Something central permeated,
spine and nerve cut through,
part of my self
                    parting from myself,
holding fast on that vast edge of the world.
The perpetual, chanting shore.

I hum what I heard.

Notes

Doubtful Sound

Doubtful Sound is at the southern tip of New Zealand. It was first discovered by Cook and labeled "Doubtful Harbour" on his map; he did not sail far enough into the opening to realize that it is a large sound. The poem is in part a found poem. The second and third stanzas are taken from Cook's journal entry for March 14, 1770, with some rearranging, some excision.

Swan-Boat Ride

The italicized words are the fragmented beginnings of a poem Elizabeth Bishop never completed. A transcribed draft is included in Alice Quinn's *Edgar Allan Poe & The Jukebox: Uncollected Poems, Drafts, and Fragments of Elizabeth Bishop* (Farrar, Straus and Giroux, 2006).

Prairie Installation

The sculptor and installation artist Andrea Lilienthal created the artwork described in this poem on the prairie behind the Ragdale house in Lake Forest, Illinois, in March/April 2014.

Lady Fishing

John Singer Sargent's painting *Lady Fishing* (1889) is at the Tate Gallery, London. Virginia Woolf no doubt saw it at some point in her life. The italicized section of the poem is taken with little alteration from Woolf's personal reminiscences *Moments of Being*.

White Garden, Kent

Many details in this poem were gleaned from Virginia Woolf's *Letters* and *Diaries*.

Acknowledgments

I would like to thank the editors of the following journals in which the following poems first appeared, sometimes in an earlier version:

The *Hudson Review* for "Woman in Kuala Lumpur";
Levure Littéraire for "April in Paris";
Ontario Review for "Colossus";
Plume for "Fresco";
Robert Frost Foundation (website) for "Red Oaks";
Sugar House Review for "Pescadero," the first section of "Starfish at Pescadero";
Valparaiso Review for "Rim";
ZYZZYVA for "Boats."

"Colman's Well" was awarded the 2015 Yeats Poetry Prize by W.B. Yeats Society of New York.

A musical setting of "Starfish at Pescadero" premiered in New York in November 2007; the contemporary chamber music group was Percussia; Dennis Tobenski was the composer; Ingrid Gordon, percussionist; and Melissa Fogarty, soprano. It has been performed several times since in various venues.

Fellowships at the MacDowell Colony, Virginia Center for the Creative Arts, and Ragdale gave me time and space to work on this manuscript. Nothing has been better for generating poems than these experiences. Endless thanks.

I honor with this collection my dear friend Diane Harmon, who has read and reread almost all of the poems I've written since I met her in 1983, who played no small role in my decision to move to the Bay Area in 1991, and who believed in me as a poet before I did. I also owe endless thanks my San Francisco Bay Area poetry group, Thirteen Ways, including Robert Thomas, Beverly Burch, Diane Kirsten-Martin, George Higgins, Zack Rogow, Melissa Stein, Lisa Gluskin Stonestreet, Jeanne Wagner, and Steven Winn—where would I be without you? Also to Dean Flower, for his encouragement and persistence; and to my dear Emily Fawcett, for her friendship and her acute observations and suggestions.

The kindness and hospitality of Edith Jones at her home on Lake Manapouri, New Zealand, made possible a day trip to Doubtful Sound, which gave me the idea for this collection. I am grateful to Dick Pesqueira and Marsha Irwin for several weeks over two summers in Dick's house at Bodega Bay, California, where a number of these poems were first drafted and revised.

I could not have traveled to so many places referenced in these poems without funding from various organizations and institutions. I am grateful to the Richard Loveland Faculty Travel Fund of Crystal Springs Uplands School which supported stays in England and Ireland. For more than two decades, CSUS was my home and my livelihood; the school provided me with extraordinary students and never stopped me from teaching poetry. I am indebted to the National Endowment for the Humanities, which funded a Summer Seminar on Virginia Woolf in London, with travel also to St. Ives, Sissinghurst, Charleston, and Rodmell. Kathy Hill-Miller designed and conducted this program of study. Continuing thanks to her for inviting me along and for that trip to The Lighthouse. Other NEH grants sent me to Harvard to study with Helen Vendler, and to Stanford to read Greek tragedy. I am grateful to the American School of Classical Studies in Athens for a summer of travel in Greece. As a consultant to The College Board, I have taught teachers in many places in the Western United States and in Kuala Lumpur. As a consultant to The Shanghai World Foreign Languages Middle School, I was able to travel to Shanghai and Suzhou, and to teach poetry.

I could not have written the poems in this book without good conversations and great travel experiences with dear friends Peggy Cornelius, Karen Dickinson, Carol Drowota, Sally Pfeifer, Louise Aliano, and Terry Canizzaro, among others. I thank Gray Holubar for his blog on Shanghai, which stimulated my thinking for "Pigs in the River"; and his father, Kent Holubar, for his excellent good-humored companionship on our trips to Shanghai and Suzhou.

I remain grateful to my mentors from the MFA Program for Writers of Warren Wilson College: Michael Collier, Reg Gibbons, Steve

Orlen, and Alan Williamson. My teacher Helen Vendler appeared at a critical time in my life; the last poem, among other muse poems in this collection, is for her.

I am also keenly aware of the loving support of my family: my sister, Lynn; my brother-in-law, Kerry; my niece, Kristin; my nephew, Tuck; and their wonderful growing families. Suzanne is my mainstay; she cooks for me, talks books with me, goes with me to concerts, plays, movies, and museums, and parents with me our two Westies, Maisie and Griffin. We have traveled together to London and England (often), France, Greece, Alaska, and New Zealand. She makes me laugh.

Finally I want to thank Sherod Santos for choosing *Doubtful Harbor* for the Hollis Summers Prize, and the good people at Ohio University Press, including Nancy Basmajian, for her eagle eye; Samara Rafert, for ushering this book into the world; and especially David Sanders—one could not hope for a better reader and editor.